God Jul ønskes Dig Harold
av Agnes Olle

Gjøvbiken den 24.12.47

INTRODUCTION

STOCKHOLM is sometimes compared, rather casually, with Venice; but though both have married land and water to make a city, the cities are distinguished not only by different architecture but by diff rent water. In Venice it is still, in Stockholm it runs. In certain places it runs very swiftly, and northern sunlight flashing on the leaping stream dresses it with such a natural gaiety as rarely characterises the highways of a large town. Stockholm, indeed, has been handsomely built, and designed with a generous regard for the appearance as well as the utility of its streets; and it is tended with loving care, as if by good gardeners and devoted housewives. But the senior partners in its charm are the gifts of nature — light and water — and in his photography Mr. Gullers has very strikingly, and most beautifully, illustrated their domination of the scene. He shows a city ruled by light and rejoicing in its streams and backwaters. He has a large variety of subjects, but the whole effect is gay, the mood is lyrical.

He catches the traffic when for a minute it is halted on a cobbled street and the cyclists poise with one foot on the pavement; he makes a singing pattern, you might almost call it a stanza, of sunlit linen hung in lines to dry; he fills a page with children leaping into a swimming-pool; he surprises an elderly lady reading her newspaper under a tree; he discovers two workmen at a paper-mill dozing on a hillock of waste paper — and in all of them, with superb craftsmanship and the artist's immediate perception of what will make a picture, there is a visible joy in the bright air and recognition of the rule of the sun.

It is a living town that Mr. Gullers presents, people at work and play in busy streets and quiet corners, and with the most artful truth he reveals the summer temper of the citizens against their material background. I turn again to photographs of a market under brilliant awnings; a girl buying flowers; a block of modern flats reflected in the water; a man painting his boat — and the illusion of reality is very strong. A lovely city has been reproduced with vivid charm, and I can think of no higher compliment than to say that Mr. Gullers has done justice to his enchanting subject.

Eric Linklater.

STOCKHOLM – The Summer City

Text by ERIK ASKLUND / Pictures by K. W. GULLERS

Published by the weekly magazine Vi

Kooperativa förbundets bokförlag, Stockholm.

Printed in Sweden by Nordisk Rotogravyr, Stockholm, 1947.

STOCKHOLM is a growing town, a great city of the future. Its population increases at the rate of about 20.000 a year, and is now nearing the 700.000 mark. In another ten years or so it will have risen to a million, nearly one-sixth of that of the entire country.

These figures sound like a great city, but the structure and characteristics of Stockholm are not quite in accordance with them. Compared with other European capitals it is still strongly reminiscent of a slightly overgrown small town, spreading swiftly out from its original core. Stockholmers feel themselves to be part and parcel of their own particular district, and in their way they can be as provincial as any of the inhabitants of the countryside. The latter are influenced by the different idiosyncrasies of their individual province, its customs or physical features, whereas the native Stockholmer is governed by a more or less developed local patriotism extending to the limits of his own district. There are families who have lived for generations in Östermalm, and who would not dream of migrating elsewhere, just as other dynasties remain equally faithful to Kungsholmen or Södermalm, despite the changes wrought by the hand of time and man in their surroundings.

Despite the march of time Stockholm has retained many original features. The ever-increasing numbers of new buildings have generally been confined to the old suburban quarters on the outskirts of the town; these have been drained and cleared and replaced by the »white cities» with their lofty apartment houses. Within the town proper, serried blocks of buildings have taken the place of the former dockyards and warehouses which used to straggle over this district. Now the surrounding waterways are walled in by a bright-hued façade, showing off to advantage the curving lines of its natural maritime boundaries. This evolution is continued over the numerous bridges leading to new forms of architecture in the shape of tower apartments, row houses or small one-family homes of a type different to those found within the town.

The central parts of the town have also undergone many changes, due to the expanding population, the varying administrative requirements and the increasing traffic, all of which demand a smoother and more modern rhythm. But here the rate of progress has been more leisurely, and glaring contrasts are still to be found in this period of transition: square white functionalistic houses elbow tumbledown hovels, narrow streets and spacious avenues run parallel to each other, the cobbled pavement is only a stone's throw from the glittering asphalt, and flowerbeds blossom in the shade of the apartment houses.

Stockholm is an ancient town. As such its name appears for the first time in the archives of 1252, though its oldest municipal privileges are of considerably later date, 1436. A tradition from 1320 ascribes its foundation to Birger Jarl. The oldest buildings and the nucleus of the city are to be found in Gamla Sta'n, the Old Town, or the Town between the Bridges as it is sometimes called. Apart from the purely historical edifices which are to be found in Gamla Sta'n, the most celebrated Stockholm buildings are of comparatively recent date. These include the Town Hall, the Kungsgatan »skyscrapers», the Law Courts, the Municipal Library and others. The new districts which are still under construction will not on the whole disturb the general aspect of the town.

But above all Stockholm is the town of its inhabitants, the town of the people. Newcomers are in the majority; for several generations there was a rapid decrease in the number of Stockholmers born, but that is now a thing of the past. The mechanism of the town is being rapidly adapted to meet the requirements of the rising population. All the vital features of a modern city are to be found here: social reforms, sanitary measures, increased comfort, swifter communications, lighter and airier living quarters, outdoor playgrounds for the children, well-tended parks, new hospitals and other institutions, up-to-date centers for pleasure, recreation and rest. But large parts of the inner town are still crowded with architectural relics of the past, with their attendant disadvantages for the inhabitants. Here sharp contrasts and social problems leap to the eye, but the underlying causes for these cannot be discussed here, as they are too complicated and closely interwoven with the political and social structure of the entire country.

This album of selected photographs depicts a summer day in Stockholm, from early dawn to nightfall, with emphasis on the human angle, man's activities and his share in the pulsating life of the city. Here the individual plays the main part, with Stockholm in the background and the wings. This book shows the town of the people at work and play: the rhythm of a single day, from the hushed dawn of awakening to the rush and bustle of a weekday noon, lunch intervals and recreation hours, to the end of the day's work, and the advent of the evening with its diversions or repose. But the face of the town has not been neglected, with its famous squares and buildings, nor its social and architectural development. Thus can it be seen through the eyes of a visiting tourist or by one of its own children, with its houses and its people, its rushing traffic, its lofty bridges and open water.

This panorama over Stockholm, the Summer City, can be epitomised in the first picture of the series, with the solitary worker passing the slumbering carts on his way from the Southern heights to the wakening town, or in the picture on the opposite page of Birger Jarl, the founder of Stockholm, standing in peaceful dignity on silent Riddarholmen.

THE TOWN IS STILL ASLEEP. The sun has just risen, dispersing the darkness of the short summer night and illuminating the panorama of the South Side with its golden beams. The green cupola of Katarina's church, the white façades of the head-offices of the Co-operative Union in the middle, the noble façades of the old mercantile palaces of Skeppsbron are revealed in the morning light, while before them the long low arch of the Skeppsholm's bridge cuts across the foreground above the rippling water.

This is the quietest hour of the day. The sun strikes sparks from the brick roofs of the ramshackle houses on the Southern heights, and the dome of the church is moss green above the sleeping windows of the houses below. The quay at Stadsgården is like a broad placid street, undisturbed by the hubbub of seaborne traffic, and the calm surface of the water is un-

flecked by foam from chattering engines. Even the gulls are at rest, snatching a respite from their indefatigable swooping and screaming. The trees are still, but small town birds are beginning to twitter in their leafy branches, and sparrows flutter inquisitively over the empty streets.

Skeppsbron is deserted, the cranes stand with dangling arms like gigantic despondent skeletons. The cloverleaf of Slussen is silent, awaiting the spinning traffic of the day. Slowly the sunlight seeks out the dark cave-like entrances to the wynds, stealing between the sullen dark houses and chasing the reluctant shadows from their crumbling walls.

The wynds are empty save for a solitary cat padding noiselessly over the cobblestones. The air is heavy with strange smells, of spices and hemp, leather and oils, dust and unwashed humanity. In another hour or two each narrow

lane will be a hotbed of sweating, shouting activity, but now they are as cool as forest ravines, peopled only by the pigeons and the sparrows upon which the cat casts such longing glances. The doors are locked on their ancient secrets, but the dawn is welcomed by the faint pipe of canaries in a cage who have felt its light penetrate the cover over their prison. Soon the sleeping inmates of the wynds will wake up to a new day. Österlånggatan lies in deep shadow, but its dusk is pierced by spears of light, as the day continues its slow inevitable siege of the slumbering houses. On the roofs surrounding Stortorget the pigeons coo their drowsy aubade to the morning. Their purple-gleaming breasts catch the light as they spread their grey wings and glide down to the cobble-stones below.

The darkness of the wynds is in vivid contrast to the unclouded brilliance of Skepps-bron, the glittering water of Strömmen, and the deeply green islet of Skeppsholmen. Farther out can be glimpsed the toy fortress of Kastellhol-men, rose-red on its hillock, like something out of an illustrated storybook. The sky is cloudless-ly blue above the Southern heights, against it the knife-sharp silhouttes of the houses look as though they had been cut out of cardboard. In another hour or two the pure blue of the sky will be stained by smoke from factory chim-neys, the silent peace jarred by shrill whistles rousing the town to work. Now the bright morning light reveals every detail of the scene with merciless clarity: the cracked stucco of the old houses, the oily sheen of the warehouse windows, the greyness of the asphalt, the silv-ery gleam of the tramlines.

In silence the city waits for man to rouse himself from his slumbers; patiently the city waits in the undisturbed radiance of the dawn.

Dawn has come to the wynd, and the rising sun pours down Brunnsgränd in Gamla Sta'n, striking the roofs of the ancient houses with its golden rays. A fisherman, his boat moored to the quay facing the Royal Palace, is busy shaking out his net, and the scavengers have assembled at Södra Station to empty their stinking cargoes into the waiting railroad cars. Flocks of hungry gulls have followed them all the way from the waterfront, in the hope of getting a free — if odoriferous — breakfast.

The town is beginning to wake up. The dustman is abroad in Gamla Sta'n, and on Strömparterren in front of the North Wing of the Palace an idler watches the fisherman setting out with his net. Gusten Lindberg's statue, the "Mist," suns her naked back with a gesture of voluptuous languor.

5.30. A bag marked Svenska Dagbladet shows that the newsboy has just gone into the house with his bundle of papers. At the corner the old man stands by his news stand, waiting for the first customers, and a train carrying the early editions thunders over the white arch of Årsta bridge on its way south.

Reveille has sounded and the soldiers of the Palace guard fold up their blankets at the Royal backdoor. The many-columned façade of the Riksdag building — the House of Parliament — glows pinkly in the morning sun behind the dark silhouette of the grim Norrbro lion. The members of the Riksdag are not in Stockholm. They have gone back to their respective provinces for the summer recess.

The world-famous view from the Grand Hotel with the Palace, the water and the little white passenger steamers. The taxi drivers stand waiting for the tourists to wake up and ring for a car. During the war foreign newspaper correspondents were the only tourists to frequent the Grand Hotel, where they made their head-quarters. Allied representatives sat cheek by jowl with their axis enemies, cabling the latest news and rumours from the tiny neutral oasis. The waiters and personnel had plenty of opportunity of practising the foreign languages which are such a necessary part of their equipment. Now the peacetime tourists are back again, and the balconied rooms at the front are at a premium once more.

The whirling currents of Strömmen — "the stream" — cut through the heart of the town. It is the chief artery of the city, leading from the broad expanses of Lake Mälaren to the Baltic, where the innumerable islands are scattered like jewels on the sea. Poets have never wearied of singing the praises of Strömmen, frozen in the cold grey light of a brief winter day, with cakes of ice floating on the ominous black surface, or as it is now, dancing past the Italianate elegance of the Opera House in veils of iridescent spray. Now the trees of the Strömparterre seem to drip honey as a gentle breeze stirs their perfumed foliage, and the ghostly shapes of seagulls drift and dive with weird echoing cries and sail arrogantly on the tumbling water. Later in the day it will be crisscrossed with stubborn little motor-boats, but now it is free and untrammelled as the solitary watcher leaning against the iron railing.

A little further on we have Kungsträdgården park, dominated by the statue of King Charles XII, the Molin fountain and an ever changing horticultural display. Kungsträdgården has its own particular place in Stockholm literature, especially that of the fin de siècle. In the days of old King Oscar it was a favourite resort of the Stockholmers of both sexes who strolled at their leisure in the shade of the elms, pausing now and again for refreshment at one of the lemonade kiosks.

Today everything is changed, and though Kungsträdgården is still a favourite rendezvous for Stockholmers with time on their hands, its former idyllic placidity is now disturbed by the clang of trams and buses on three sides and the flow of motor traffic from Arsenalsgatan. But the bells of Jakob's church still peal forth as before, fashionable weddings are still celebrated there and the Operakällaren restaurant is only a few steps away.

A summer morning on Vintervägen, the Winter Way. The market folk outside Klarahallen are beginning to set up their stalls. Trucks come rolling in from the country with their cargo of flowers, fruit and vegetables. They begin to arrive at four in the morning when the inmates of the tall white tenement houses in the background are still sound asleep. The crates are unpacked and the trestle tables are soon covered with tubs of brilliant flowers, and mounds of jade and ivory cauliflowers. Punnets of scarlet strawberries and the deeper crimson of raspberries contrast with the clear green of cucumbers and melons. Soon the buyers arrive and a new fleet of cars stands waiting to be loaded with their purchases.

There is a fruit market within the hall as well, but out here in the open, under the tall red spire of the Town Hall, it is more lively, almost Southern. The buyers chaffer and haggle, the sellers protest, maintaining the superior quality of their wares and the cheapness of their prices. The purchases are mostly wholesale, made by fellow tradesmen, flower-shop-owners, representatives of restaurants and large retailers. A little later on, stray customers put in a belated appearance, housewives on the lookout for special strawberries in the jam-making season, vegetables or fruit for bottling. Artists drop in to choose an armful of mixed flowers for their next still life, and young men in love buy roses for the lady of their choice.

Nearly every Stockholmer has a boat of sorts. A careful owner is repainting his, while above his head the traffic roars over Västerbron. The steam locomotive is shunting its loaded trucks on the railway lines which connect Stadsgården with the quay at Söder Mälarstrand. The lock gates have just been closed for an outgoing tug on its way to Stadsgården. The road and water traffic of the city is under way.

The first bicyclists are on their way to work along tidy Ringvägen, passing Södersjukhuset, Stockholm's newest hospital. The shops are beginning to open, the owners polish the windows and arrange their wares to the best advantage. The pavement comes in for its share of cleaning. The coal shovel vomits its black load from the bunker into the barge lying alongside the grey freighter in the Hammarby Channel.

Holiday makers have already started queueing up at the barrier in the Central Station. This queue is waiting for the southgoing express which will take them to the beaches of Skåne and Halland. Young and old, they stand with their coats over their arms and their suitcases beside them. They come in good time so as to make sure of a seat in the crowded train, and the main hall is a relatively cool and pleasant spot in which to while away the minutes before the ticket collector lets them through to the platform. In the meantime they are kept busy counting their children and their luggage, their keys and their tickets.

The early morning traffic rolls forward in two serried ranks, heading for the centre of the town. The red light flickers at Tegelbacken level crossing. Behind the lowered barrier the arrested line of traffic extends as far back as the Town Hall. It is a quarter to nine, the rush hour for office workers, the bicyclists wind their way through the medley of cars and buses towards the head of the line. A goods train puffs across the level crossing towards the Central Station. The tower of the Town Hall glows dully crimson against the blue of the sky and the green of the leaves, standing sentinel in the background.

Stockholm is a city of contrasts. It can happen that the modern thoroughfares have their poor relations, slinking along beside them in the shadow of their grandeur. They are narrower, the cobblestones of their pavements have been worn down by many generations of stumbling feet, and the relentless centuries have scooped hollows in the stone doorsteps. The jangle of the trams and the roar of the buses come as a faint echo to these shabby houses whose windows are often bright with potted geraniums or the tortured green flesh of cacti, and whose backyards resound with children's voices.

Västerlånggatan is the main street of the Old Town, its narrow roadway is constantly blocked with cars and the old houses have been transformed into shops, their plateglass windows ablaze with wares of every kind. It is the oldest shopping center in Stockholm and it has many loyal customers in the Old Town who prefer it to Regeringsgatan or Kungsgatan on the other side of the bridges. Västerlånggatan has a poor relation, Prästgatan, with which it is connected by the numerous narrow wynds which intersect the entire district. Prästgatan is dark and mysterious, no sunshine can entirely disperse the shadows from the tall houses which make such a brave display in Västerlånggatan, but who have their true faces turned the other way, towards Prästgatan. They are old and worn, nobody has bothered to repaint the cracked and peeling walls, or to mend the creaking doors and windows, but the inhabitants make a valiant attempt to enliven their sordid homes with a few cheerful touches. Gay cotton curtains veil the eternal potted plants, and a child has hung out a national flag from the first floor window. But Prästgatan is not a place in which to walk alone at night, and even now with the sunlight flooding in and tearing down the darkest veils it is very like a deep channel winding its way secretively over the narrow alleys which traverse it, never quite revealing what lies at its bottom. It runs from Storkyrkobrinken to Österlånggatan, dogging the gaudy lively Västerlånggatan like a sinister phantom of the past, an inexhaustible well of memories from the dead and gone centuries.

But the wynds around Stortorget are full of life and bustle. A magnificent Boxer exchanges a last word with his master on his way to work. The church angel gazes down from her perch in the curiosity shop window, and the imposing stone doorways from a bygone age serve a more practical purpose than that for which they were built. One leads to a dairy shop and another is thrown open to admit the carter with his sack of firewood. Above them all looms the belfry of Storkyrkan, the great church.

The morning rush is at its liveliest near Slussen. A swarm of humanity emerges from the suburban line station at Södermalmstorg, on their way to work. Above their heads the Katarina lift reaches its long arm to the head-offices of the Cooperative Union. This is an important traffic center, suburban buses and trams, the Saltsjöbaden trains, and innumerable cars and ferries all meet here, and the vehicles spin round over and under ground, sorting themselves out according to their various destinations.

Another important center is Tegelbacken, at which many blocks and stoppages occur round about nine o'clock. A double line of traffic is waiting on the lower street level for the green signal to shine ahead at Vasagatan, after which — if lucky — it may be able to proceed for a few more yards before being stopped again. But this is a pleasant halting place with the green trees spreading their branches over the old stone wall, and the sparkling water on the other side of the bustling clamorous street.

Nine o'clock. Office work is in full swing, but the shoppers have not yet begun their rounds, and the shops are still preparing for the day. Wire cages of empty milk bottles are stacked on to a lorry and the wholesale baker has just arrived with wooden boxes full of fresh bread. Fat shining bream is offered for sale at the fish market by Kornhamnstorg, and the trucks at the meat market in Munkbrogatan are piled high with slaughtered pigs. The stevedores in Hammarby harbour are taking time off for a well-earned snooze among the scattered paper bales which did not survive the unloading.

Around Klara church lie the newspaper offices; this is the head-quarters of the Swedish press. Now is the time to get things in order for tomorrow's editions. Huge rolls of paper are prepared for the printing machines. Fortunately Sweden is the land of paper, so there is normally no shortage of material but the demands are enormous, and a roll like this one is quickly devoured. The first traffic rush is over, and the tramline workers can weld the rails and repair the tracks without being unduly disturbed.

Norra Bantorget is one of the liveliest traffic centers in the town, but its chief claim to fame is the large building in the background with its twin turrets; the head-quarters of the labour unions. Its political opponents have nicknamed it "the Vatican", and many important decisions affecting the prosperity of the entire country, have taken place within its walls. The great square outside has a place of its own in the annals of Swedish Socialism. Every May 1st, the red flags are unfurled as the workers' procession marches past on its way to the open space at Gärdet where the annual demonstrations are held. The Social Democratic party paper now calls itself Morgon-Tidningen and has moved from Folkets Hus in Barnhusgatan, but that citadel of the Swedish Labour movement is still the centre of much activity. Many discussions are held in the hall downstairs around the bronze statue of the worker, by Meunier, and theatrical performances as well as political meetings take place in the auditorium. Its somewhat shabby interior holds many memories for the champions of the people who now have witnessed the triumph of their cause.

KLÄDMOTTAGNING FÖR SAL. A

TEATER   Ingen handel får förekomma i hallen

There are practically no beggars in Stockholm, but the streets are full of workers who exercise their profession out of doors. Flower sellers extol the merits of their wares, and compete with the fruit vendor at the next corner. In a doorway an elderly man sells the lists of winning lottery numbers; he is sure of getting the same customers month after month, for it would be difficult to find a Swede who has not bought at least part of a lottery ticket or invested fifty kronor in a State Savings bond which gives him a biannual chance of winning from twentyfive to two hundred thousand kronor.

Here is an asphalt cart which has come to a halt in the middle of Drottninggatan, one of the busiest streets in the center of the town. The sharp scent of the smoking asphalt makes the passers-by cough and hurry on their way to the latest summer sale, but the road-mender is hardened to it. He stirs it with his iron rod as though it were a gigantic Christmas pudding. Black bubbles rise to the surface and sink back again into the steaming mass. In the meantime the roadmender surveys the street with an expert eye, looking for traces of wear in the asphalt paving. His job is to mend the holes which result from the heavy traffic, and as soon as he finds one he tilts his container and lets a slow tarry avalanche roll down over it. Then he climbs down from his perch and goes down on his hands and knees to smooth it out. Buses lurch round him, messenger boys skim past on their bicycles, but he continues tranquilly with his work from one end of the long street to the other.

The old knife grinder has established himself in the sun by Hötorget, one of the city's open air markets, where he is sure of many customers. There is a covered market near by, and the women there have plenty of opportunity of blunting their cutlery. He goes his rounds once or twice a week, edging his way through the crowds round the stalls and comes back to his grinding machine with his hands full of knives and scissors. Slowly, with the unhurried certainty of long years of experience, he tests each blade against his thumb before subjecting it to the grindstone.

The broad highway of Kungsgatan cuts through three sections of the city, beginning at Stureplan in Östermalm, and continuing across Norrmalm to Kungsholmen. It is the biggest shopping street in the town and many world-famous concerns have their headquarters in Kungsgatan. Here also is the Concert House, several cinemas and Oscar's Theatre. One of the largest buildings belongs to PUB, a leading department store, whose plate glass windows dominate an entire block with a never-ending stream of traffic.

Karlaplan is the playground for the children of Östermalm. Here are sandpits and switchbacks and the pool in the center is a never-failing source of delight, winter and summer. At Christmas the fountain ceases to play and is replaced by a gigantic Christmas tree, covered with twinkling lights, and many skaters have had their first falls on the ice at Karlaplan. In the background can be seen the red brick turrets of No. 10, where August Strindberg lived, and which is the scene of his famous play The Ghost Sonata.

Luncheon hour. Two typists have taken a parcel of sandwiches with them to the office and are eating them in the sunshine on the quay on Riddarholmen, overlooking Söder Mälarstrand.

On the other side of the water two workmen descend the stone steps of Maria Trappgränd on their way back to their job.

But the two dockers on the terrace of the old Riddarholm café linger over their coffee, though their comrades on the quay below are hard at work loading the white Mälar lake steamer with a motley collection of crates and sacks and packages on their way out to the verdant islands, the glittering creeks, the sleeping cities like Mariefred and Strängnäs, the industrial towns such as Västerås and Eskilstuna.

During the summer the Riddarholm quay comes to life again and there is always a certain amount of bustle at the arrival and departure of the Mälar steamers, which now carry passengers to the islands and summer resorts as well as cargo, but the winter ice puts a stop to all this, and Riddarholmen seems to drop back to sleep again. This is one of the oldest parts of Stockholm: the most ancient building, the Wrangel palace, is to be found on this island, and so are the Svea Hovrätt (Court of Appeal) and the State Archives. According to the Erik chronicles, Riddarholmen was originally called Kidaskär, or the Island of the Kids, being used as pasture land. Later, about 1268, a monastery was founded there and the name was changed to Gråmunkeholmen. Many famous Swedes saw the light of day on this island, including the renowned dramatist August Strindberg.

Riddarholmen is dominated by its mighty church which houses the tombs of the Vasa Kings among others. It is a district of picturesque corners, winding streets and sudden entrancing views where the green heights of Söder reflected in blue water, burst unexpectedly on the wanderer from round the next corner.

It is quieter and more reserved than Gamla Sta'n, as though wrapped in the mantle of its past memories.

The view from Björns Trädgård presents a panorama of the latest political, commercial and communal developments in the life of the city. From left to right we have Medborgarhuset, the head-quarters of the Co-operative Society and Söder hospital. On the opposite page the tall white building called the Women's House rears itself into the air. Here single professional women live in modern airy apartments, which glaringly contrast with the fifty year old wooden houses below them.

Stockholm is a city of sun worshippers. The winter is so very long and the summer so tragically short; every hour of sunshine must be utilized to the utmost. This old lady has taken a tram to Djurgården and is having a picnic meal of coffee and sandwiches on the grass under the trees with her newspaper.

The girls under K. G. Scheele's statue have not gone so far afield: they are taking their sunbath on Flora's Mound in Humlegården park. The 18th century scientist seems to be speculating on the trend in modern fashions, or perhaps he is indicating which pair of legs takes the prize for symmetry and sunburn.

CARL MICHAEL
BELLMAN

The Djurgårdsbrunn canal is much frequented by small privately owned motorboats, chugging over its quiet waters on their way to the archipelago or the open sea. Their rush hours are on Saturday afternoon and again on Sunday evening when they bustle back to town. The passengers are in such a hurry to reach their destination that they can hardly spare a glance for the magnificent old oaks which line their pathway or the flower-starred grass sloping down to the stone banks. And yet this is one of the loveliest spots in Stockholm, winter and summer alike, when the first green buds appear in spring or when the October leaves blaze gold and red.

Now in July the lime trees fill the air with honey-sweet fragrance, and the busy hum of the bees is like a sordino accompaniment to the discant of birdsong. Those Stockholmers who cannot leave the town spend much time in Djurgården, but it is so spacious that it is possible to roam in it as undisturbed as though one were in a private park. The bust of Carl Michael Bellman, Sweden's best beloved poet and composer, looks over a typical grove, surrounded with trees. Every year on July 26, Bellman's memory is celebrated in Djurgården by a rococo carnival.

Around Djurgården are various museums, many fine houses, of which the Spanish and Italian Legations, formerly the property of Royal Princes, and Prince Eugen's Waldemarsudde are the most outstanding, and above all, Skansen. The latter is a combination of outdoor museum and entertainment park. During the summer open air concerts are given at which leading Swedish artists perform. But the most popular section of Skansen is undoubtedly the zoo. Practically every year one or other of the bears produces a new pair of twins, which never fail to draw a public of all ages. Here the babies have managed to conceal themselves behind one of the boulders of their rocky home and their mother, blasé as a film star, turns her back to the audience and gazes out into space. She may be dreaming of her Norrland home, but her eyes are fixed on the gasworks and the ultra modern apartment houses of Gärdet.

But Djurgården is something more than a verdant pleasure park. Down on the water side, we have the shipyards, the noisy Galärvarv which is devoted to the upkeep and reparation of naval vessels of every description. A worker is busy welding a davit against the background of Nordiska Museum, whose green copper dome and slender spire tower high above the struts and stays.

The Djurgård ferry takes one over to Skeppsbron, opposite the Seamen's Agency. Two merchant seamen, an elderly stoker and a young deckhand, are standing on its steps, waiting for a job. In front of them lies Strömmen with its swarm of craft. A tramp steamer is laid upon the stocks while its propeller is repaired. Out in the Free Harbour at Värtan a graceful three-masted schooner is discharging her cargo of cement. Many young seamen make their first trips aboard a sailingship.

Tegelbacken and Stureplan are two of the busiest spots in Stockholm, where the traffic problem is shown at its worst, and the humble pedestrian is obliged to have all his wits about him. Tegelbacken is the starting place and terminus for the trams which serve the garden suburbs. The lines to Lidingö and Djursholm start near Stureplan, which is in the heart of fashionable Stockholm. Here the most distinguishing feature is the so-called "mushroom", a favourite rendezvous as well as a shelter from unexpected showers.

The fruit and flowers in the market stands on Hötorget have been partially covered by striped awnings
to protect them from the noonday sun. Carl Milles'
Orpheus strikes his lyre on the steps of the Concert
House. Another openair market is that at Östermalms-
torg. A summer-clad girl discusses begonias with the
elderly seller, with traffic streaming by in the background, concealing Hedvig Eleonora church behind.

But the day's work is not yet over. In Stadsgården the dockers roll motor tyres like giant hoops across the quay. The sunlit harbour is walled in by the blackness of the primitive rock cliff.

It is recreation time for some of the hardworking hospital nurses. They take a tram from their headquarters at Sabbatsberg hospital and go to Haga for a cup of coffee and a cake on a café verandah.

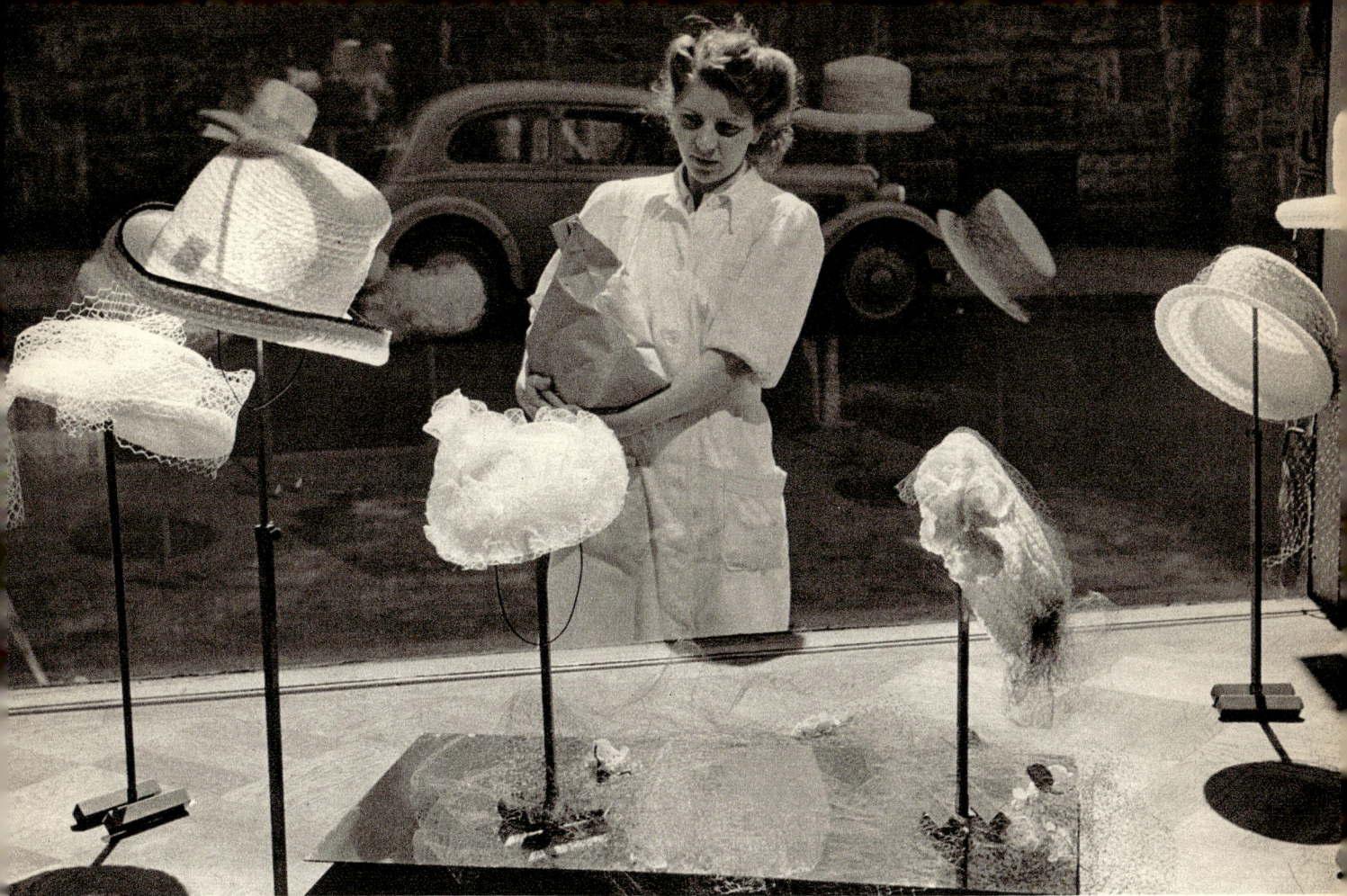

A shopgirl from the oil and colourman's store pauses to admire the latest fashions in summer hats wondering which of the frivolous Paris models she would choose if she were to draw a winning number.

A horse has cast a shoe in the middle of Vasagatan in front of the General Post Office, and is holding up the traffic while his driver unhurriedly repairs the damage. Neither of them appears to suffer from nerves.

Söder Mälarstrand is nearly as sandy as the Sahara. In the old days a working gang used to go out consisting of half a dozen men with wheelbarrows, now the same quantity of sand is shifted in a fraction of the time by a steam shovel and a lorry.

The same crane attends to the unloading of the barges by the quayside, worked by a single man who surveys the scene from his eyrie before pressing down the levers. The present methods seem almost nonchalant in comparison with those of the past, but they are infinitely more effective, to say nothing of the immense saving in manpower.

Söder Mälarstrand is part of the extensive quay system which lines all the waterways of Stockholm. Lighters and barges tie up here, laden with gravel, cement, sand and brick. They fetch their cargoes from Lake Mälaren, from the gravel pits far up in Björköfjärden, from the brick kilns in the Mälar valley, the stone quarries of far off Bohuslän and the lime kilns in the Stockholm archipelago.

Söder Mälarstrand is covered with huge sand heaps, mountains of red bricks and thousands of sacks of cement lying in rows along the edge of the quay all of which are destined to contribute to the construction of new buildings far away from the center of the town. They will be transformed into modern apartment houses or into gleaming white factories, like the Luma works on the other side of Hammarby Channel.

SE UPP
GÅ EJ UNDER LAST I
KRANKROK ELLER
GRIPSKOPA

LYFT

In the crowd of passers-by an occasional face stands out and lingers in the memory. Judging from the decorative tattooing on his arm the lorrydriver started his career as a seaman. The typesetter wears a distinctive cap, and the uniforms of the nurse and the postman are unmistakable. The carefree errand boy whistling past on his bicycle is a feature of every European city, and his repertoire is often the same.

Stockholm is a town with many points of vantage, but the man on the bollard underneath the railway bridge seems more interested in his newspaper than in the beautiful silhouette of the Town Hall on the other side of Riddarfjärden. Farther on is the pictures-que Petersen house, dating from the middle of the 17th century. Munkbron opposite used to be the scene of a Midsummer carnival, one of the annual high-lights. It is still celebrated with improvised music and dancing, but minus the vigour of bygone days.

Modern Stockholm is a city of tall white houses with great expanses of window and numerous balconies. They mirror themselves in the still waters of the Klara Canal, and crown the rocky hilltops of Reimersholme.

These functionalistic dwelling-houses are nearly all of comparatively recent date and have not yet ousted the little red cottages which are still to be found on the outskirts of the city. In fact some of the most modern tenements are in unpleasantly close proximity to areas which can almost be described as slums, which have long ago been theoretically condemned as unfit for habitation, but which still have their inmates, for like all other capitals, rapidly expanding Stockholm suffers from an acute housing problem. But the modern houses are in the majority and it is only a matter of time before the picturesque wooden shacks become a mere memory.

The more central parts of the town change their aspect almost from day to day. The HSB cooperative housing organization is responsible for extensive building projects at Kungsholmen and Södermalm. Gärdet, beyond Östermalm, has expanded to the limit, and the new suburb on the other side of Skanstullsbro, the latest addition to the bridges of Stockholm, is now the city's most rapidly growing section.

This HSB, or Tenants' Savings and Building Society, is today by far the largest cooperative housing society in Sweden, and during the past few years it has been responsible for 12—13 % of the total house-building activity in the country. It is confidently expected that the activity will be expanded still further in the near future, combating the scourge of overcrowding.

The shining white houses are poised on the heights of Reimersholme like lighthouses welcoming a new era. The rock on which they stand was once the scene of the annual Walpurgis Eve bonfire (April 30), whose flames were visible all over the town. Now from the expansive windows the inmates can see similar abodes as far west as Mälardalen and east to Klippan by Danvikstull, while at their feet the waterways of Stockholm wind peacefully among the leafy trees.

The old Strömbad by the railroad bridge is a thing of the past. It was a relic of the time when the dwellers on Lake Mälaren used its waters for all kinds of washing and bathing. Now the roof of Strömsborg restaurant has been reserved for sunbathers. The quicksilver creeps up to a dizzy altitude here, and the roof is always thick with ardent sunworshippers.

Another popular spot is Vanadis open air bath in the heart of the city, with its large pool and comfortable lounging benches alongside. Young and old flock here in large numbers to splash in the cool water or toast themselves on the scorching tiles. Planted like a shelf in the park hillside this pool insulates itself against the city traffic roaring below.

Even the smallest parks and squares in Stockholm have been adapted as children's playgrounds. Swings and roundabouts, seesaws and switchbacks are at their disposition as well as a good-natured "lektant" or games organizer whose task it is to see that the children all have a good time. She keeps an eye on the smaller ones and sees that they are not unduly bullied by their seniors, and gets up round games, thereby giving mothers a well-earned rest. The little girl who is seeking refreshment at the drinking fountain, does not look as though she were pining away for lack of fresh air and exercise, despite her summer in town.

The City Library is the building which really marks the beginning of the transition from traditional to modern architecture in Sweden. Built in 1928, it nestles against the green slopes of Observatorielunden. The Library occupies an entire block at the corner of Sveavägen and Odengatan and it contains books in every language on every subject. Many of the readers are absent at this time of year, when so many Stockholmers are on holiday, but there is always a steady stream of borrowers passing up the broad shallow steps. There is also a newspaper room, where the whole national press may be studied as well as many foreign periodicals, and this is never empty.

The houses on Norr Mälarstrand are mostly of the same date. They extend from Kungsholmstorg to Västerbron, and the little green path which winds along the lake front here is much appreciated by summer strollers, when they take their evening walk.

The summer holidays are in full swing, and these boys from the South Side have organized their amusements from start to finish. First they collect their bait, digging up worms in Klara cemetery by the light of pocket flashlamps, quite unimpressed by their awe-inspiring surroundings; they sell some of their treasure-trove to the nearest ironmonger or sports outfitters, reserving enough for their day's fishing on the quays. The harbour here is almost covered with craft of every description, but there is always a chance of sport even in these crowded waters, and like all fishermen they are confirmed optimists.

There are boys like these in every town, who do not go to the Children's Colonies in the archipelago, who do not seem to have any relations in the country who can invite them to spend the holidays there. But it is doubtful whether they suffer from this seeming neglectfulness. They have such fun at home in Stockholm, roaming the docks and exploring the ships in the harbour. They get free trips in the tugs and ferryboats as far as the Free Harbour or to Henriksdal; they are as familiar with the waterways of Stockholm as they are with the back streets of their native South Side. It is quite possible that they are not among the shining lights of the class-room, but they are experts in picking up unconsidered trifles in the customs sheds or on the quayside. Sometimes they earn a little money by running errands, generally connected with bottles of beer, for some of the stevedores. It is quite possible that none of them will ever master German verbs, but already, they are at home in the lingua franca of the sea. They may not get high marks in geography but they know the markings of all the ships in the harbour, and the different cargoes which they bring and carry away with them.

But just now all their attention is concentrated on a fat bream which has finally decided to make a snap at their bait. The long hours of patient and fruitless angling will reap their well merited reward, when they triumphantly succeed in hauling their slippery prize ashore.

The children use Johannes' churchyard as a playground, and the little girl's skipping rope whirls round in the shadow of the tombstones. The old pensioners from the neighbouring almshouses stroll slowly in the sunshine with their backs to the soaring red spire.

Johannes' cemetery has many literary associations. Stockholm writers, from Hjalmar Söderberg to Agnes von Krusenstjerna and Gunnar Ekelöf, have used it as a background in their books. Georg von Döbeln, the hero of Sweden's last war in 1809, is buried here with his life's motto as epitaph: Honour, Duty, Determination, and a simple gravestone marks the last resting place of Gunilla Bjelke: »Louis De Geer's beloved Wife».

This cheerful band of youngsters is on its way home from Flaten lake outside Stockholm. The municipal sports committee has organized a service of buses and trams which go the round of the city in the morning, collecting children of all ages, from toddlers up to fourteen-year-olds, at various fixed stopping places. They are then driven out to Flaten bathing beach where competent superintendents are in charge of the visitors. They are given buns and fruit drinks, games are organized under the pine trees, and swimming lessons are an important part of the program.

Many of these children come from the narrow alleys and backyards of the old town, where the sun seldom penetrates, from old-fashioned insanitary homes, where their only playground is the crowded noisy street or the parched parks the air of which is heavy with petrol fumes from the surrounding streets. In contrast with these Flaten is a paradise, and their overworked mothers look upon it as a valuable substitute for the country holiday to which all cannot aspire.

The end of the summer ought to find these children sunburned and healthy with a store of accumulated vitamins with which to face the long dark winter which lies ahead of them.

Somebody has had a major washing day, and the back yard is festooned with trophies of the washtub. Sheets, towels and dusters flap like white flags in the air, filling it with a clean soapy scent. This phalanx of backyards forms the meetingplace of the inmates of the tall houses on either side. Here carpets are beaten, and the smaller children have their playgrounds where their mothers can keep an eye on them through the open kitchen window. The potted plants beloved of every Swedish housewife are carried out to profit from an occasional summer shower and compared with those of the neighbours, but the smell of geraniums and newly laundered linen does not predominate as a rule. Pride of place is claimed by the ever present garbage cans, not to speak of the culinary odours which stream through the kitchen windows, advertising the meatballs or herring of the day's dinner.

Every summer afternoon there is a crowd waiting for the archipelago steamers down at Nybroviken and Karl XII's Torg, but on Saturday it is almost impossible to get standingroom on board. All Stockholm seems to be on its way to the archipelago, excepting those who prefer to explore the creeks and islets of Lake Mälaren with their own motorboats or small sailing craft. The lofty concrete arch of Traneberg bridge spans the arm of the lake, supporting a main arterial highway.

The working day has come to an end. The whistle has given the order *Down Tools!* all over the dockyard, and the workers leave the ocean-going freighter they are building and tramp down the gangway on their way home. Their first port of call is the washroom where they take a shower to get rid of the oil and soot, change from their dungarees into ordinary clothes, and so home to supper, the evening paper, and a well-earned snooze in an easy chair to the strains of the radio program.

The eight-hour day has been a strenuous one, riveting, welding, hammering away at the hull of the big vessel which has been laid up to undergo inspection and the necessary repairs after all the years of idleness and inactivity during the war. The little white steamers leave Nybroviken and chug their way out towards the archipelago, their decks black with passengers. Coils of smoke wreathe themselves round the empty hulls as the smouldering coals burn slowly out in the furnaces.

Soon the dockyard lapses into silence. Only the watchman goes his rounds, making his way between beams and stays, all the apparent confusion of giant wires and cordage which goes to the making of a ship. The stillness is broken only by the lapping of the water against the hulls.

The workers have passed through the dock gates. Some have their bicycles waiting for them in the parking places outside, others live near enough to walk home, others wait for a bus or tram.

All categories are to be found on Stureplan, waiting for one of the trolleybuses to take them home to Kungsholmen, or alternatively Gärdet. The number of private car-owners has never been very large, and in the summer Stockholmers generally prefer the bicycle as a means of locomotion.

Everywhere the scene is the same. A steady stream of factory workers issues from the gates of Luma, L. M. Ericsson, Aga, and a dozen other factories whose products are known the world over. The trams and buses are filled to overflowing, the bicycles jostle each other on the street.

The offices release their typists and accountants, who rush to do a little marketing before joining the homeward bound procession. The girls make a detour along the shopping thoroughfares of Kungsgatan and Hamngatan in order to flatten their noses against the window-panes, perhaps even to succumb to temptation, if it is the beginning of the month, and dart in to try on an irresistible hat or frock before the big department stores lock their plateglass doors and their staff emerge from smaller doorways giving on the back streets. The refuges are black with pedestrians waiting for a chance to plunge through the traffic and reach the other side, or wondering whether they will be able to get a seat or even standingroom on the next tram.

Extra cars and buses run during the rush hours, but they barely suffice, for all over Stockholm and around it, the scene is the same: workers of every description, their day's toil over, homeward bound.

Sport plays a large part in the Stockholmer's life. Some enthusiastic runners are here training at Zinkensdamm, one of the many modern sportsgrounds available in the city.

But these lads are not alone in their energy and athletic interests. The housewives of Sockholm have been assembled together by their enthusiastic leader, Elly Löfstrand, and induced to indulge in gymnastics. Their first attempts were made at Zinkensdamm with a nucleus of seventeen heroic women. Now housewives' gymnastics has become a national institution and the forerunner of similar activities abroad.

The rush hours are between four and six. After that there is a pause in the traffic, before the pleasure seeking crowds go abroad again, on their way to cinema, theatre or concert. The shops are shut, and the streets are almost empty. The market folk have packed up and gone home, and Hötorget is being swept clean in preparation for the morrow. Orpheus is in the shade, the sunbeams no longer strike his gleaming bronze shoulders as he soars upwards from the ring of bemused mortals at his feet. The plash of the fountain round his pedestal is clearly audible in the unaccustomed stillness. The steps of the Concert House, a favourite spot in the lunch hour for sun-worshippers, are almost unoccupied, only a few idlers remain at the foot of its stylized Corinthian pillars, regardless of the dust which whirls around them.

An errand boy comes home to Söder, making his last delivery of cakes and buns on the way. The wooden box which contained them will go back to the baker with him tomorrow morning. His home is in Pryssgränd, near Slussen, an obscure, little-known street with low old-fashioned houses. The evening sun lights up some of them, and an appetising smell of cooking streams out of the open windows.

This is one of the many almost provincial corners of Stockholm which escape the attention of the average tourist, and the majority of the inhabitants are probably unaware of its existence.

Dusk falls over the city, as the long summer day draws to a close. One by one the lights go up, their bright globes contrasting with the fading daylight. The sun has gone down beyond Väster-bron, and Norr Mälarstrand glitters like a necklace of gems. The tower of the Town Hall is silhouetted against the darkening sky. The shadowy outline of Riddarholmen clustering round the tall dark spire of Riddarholmskyrkan is sprinkled with lamps, while the business districts are fairly ablaze with neon lights. The shop windows still show a display of temptingly arranged goods of various kinds, cinemas blazon their programs with the names of the stars in man-sized lettering. The verandahs of the restaurants are bright with fairy lanterns, luring the passers-by to stop and eat their dinner in such festive surroundings. As an extra temptation, the menus are hung outside the doors.

Gamla Sta'n huddles together in the darkness, the wynds are inky tunnels lit by a single lamp swinging on a wire strung across the street. Here too there are famous restaurants, such as Gyldene Freden or Bacchi Wapen, but many more humble cafés where dockhands drop in to drink a glass of beer and study the sports pages in the evening paper.

From the heights of the Katarina lift we look down on Södermalmstorg, almost unrecognisable in its idleness. An occasional tram clanks leisurely past, and small groups of people cross what was a maelstrom of traffic an hour or two ago, scarcely troubling to look to the right or left. They are on their way out to play. Stockholm has plenty to offer on a summer night, the restaurants and fun fairs of Djurgården, and nume-rous outdoor cafés for the less energe-tic. Not to speak of Skansen and of the public parks such as Berzelii park and Vasaparken, where orchestras perform every evening during the warm season.

An occasional boat twinkles down Strömmen on its way back from the archipelago, filled with tired and sun-burned holidaymakers.

The worst of the heat disappears with the sun and a soft breeze blows in from the open sea.

Tram number 7 leaves its starting place at Norrmalmstorg and glides down Strandvägen to Djurgården. To many young Stockholmers, it is the most exciting tram in town as it swings to the right across the bridge to pass a concourse of pedestrians on their way to the various restaurants and places of amusement in the park. The narrow bridge is black with cyclists and cars and the paths beneath the scented limes are thronged with strollers. They have plenty of choice, classical music up on the heights of Skansen, of dancing to a jazz orchestra in the open air, an hour at the circus, a meal at one of the numerous restaurants under a gaily striped sun parasol, or a turn at the fun fair.

There are two of the latter, facing each other in Allmänna Gränd, their neon lights rivalling each other as they proclaim their star attractions. Opera stars singing the most appealing arias in their repertoire, acrobats performing high above the heads of the public with the star-strewn sky as a back cloth, jugglers, magicians and dancers — you can take your choice between Gröna Lunds Tivoli and Nöjesfältet. Then there are shooting galleries, fortune tellers, swings and roundabouts, all the paraphernalia of a well-equipped amusement park.

A steady stream of customers flows through the turnstiles, or stands waiting outside for their partners for the evening, and inside shrieks of excitement as the giant swing hangs upside down above the heads of the public mingle with the wailing saxophones by the dance pavilion. The Navy provides a large proportion of the patrons, wandering with unflagging energy from the Haunted House to the Caves of Mystery and the Giant Switchback, generally with a girl on each arm. Stockholm amuses itself whole-heartedly and full-throatedly on this side of Djurgården. Then when the last shot echoes in the shooting galleries and the last glittering prize is presented to the winning marksman, when the booths are closed and the lights lowered, then the hoarse but happy merrymakers stroll arm in arm over the bridge and back to the slumbering town.

SILENTLY the brief summer night invades the city. The last faint glow has left the western sky, but in another hour or two it will begin to reappear in the east, for twilight and dawn are very near neighbours at this time of year. The last night-wanderers begin to wend their way home, the restaurants and fun fairs have closed their doors, and the trams and buses have ceased their clangour.

But though the town is still, it is not utterly asleep, just as the darkness never really enfolds it. The outlines of the roofs and steeples are clearly visible against the soft grey of the sky; the lamps of Västerbron are like a string of topazes against a background of velvet; and Engelbrekt raises his banner of liberty for all to see.

Somebody is always awake, on the watch, waiting. The taxi drivers snatch forty winks while waiting for the telephone to ring at their station; the policemen and night watchmen faithfully go their rounds; and a band of workmen are busy repairing a tramway line by the light of dull red lamps and their own flashing tools.

The long day is over, its clamour and bustle have died away, but the turmoil of a new one is only just round the corner.

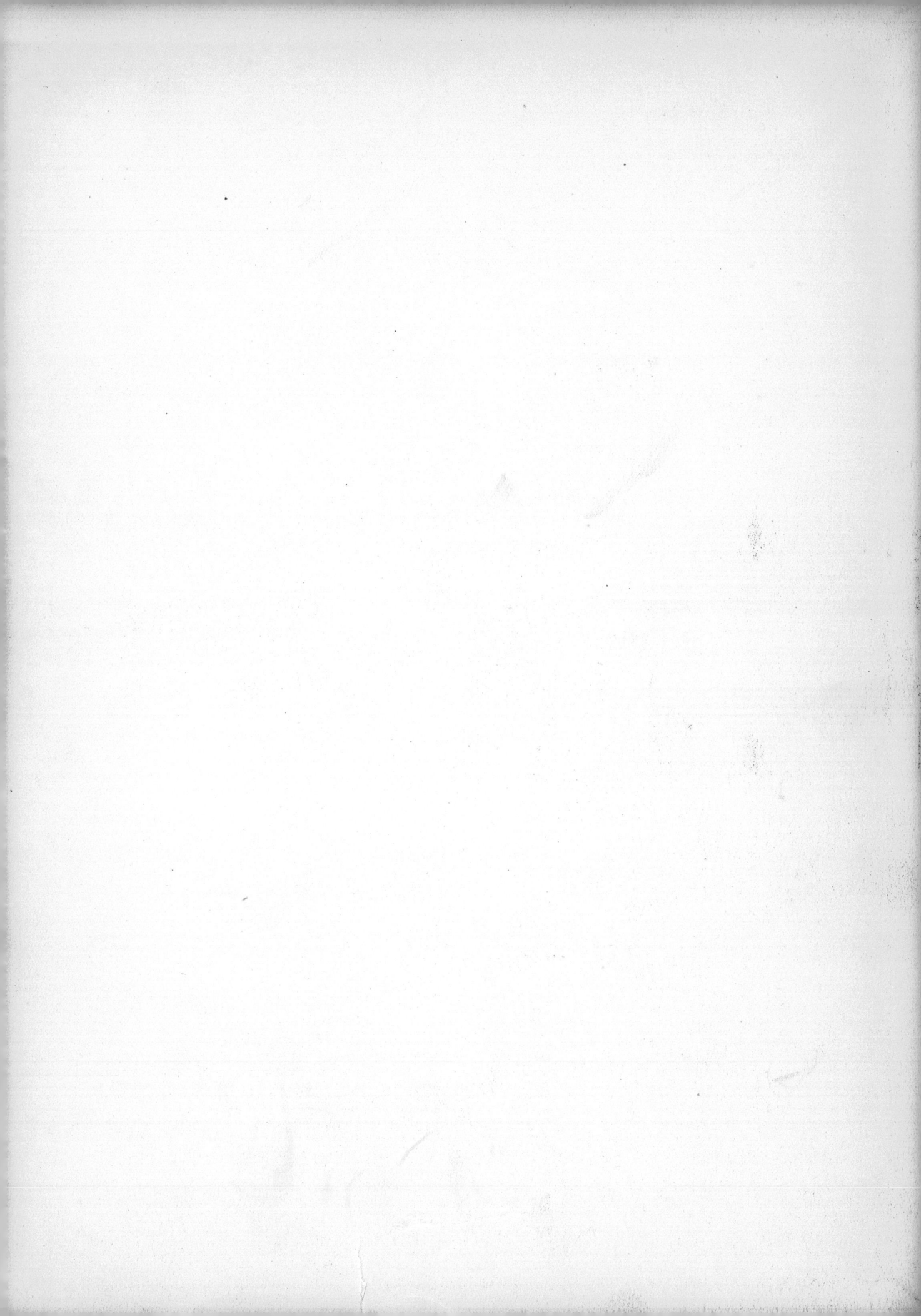